TUNiTY

iNDNESS

NOWLEDGE

TUNiTY

RATEGY

TUNiTY

W9-BLA-364

SCORE!

50 Poems to Motivate and Inspire

by Charles Ghigna   illustrated by Julia Gorton

ABRAMS

BOOKS FOR YOUNG READERS, NEW YORK

Library of Congress Cataloging-in-Publication Data:

Ghigna, Charles.
Score! : 50 poems to motivate and inspire / by Charles Ghigna ;
illustrated by Julia Gorton.
p. cm.
ISBN-13: 978-0-8109-9488-1
ISBN-10: 0-8109-9488-7
1. Success—Juvenile poetry. 2. Conduct of life—Juvenile poetry.
3. Children's poetry, American. I. Gorton, Julia, ill. II. Title.

PS3557.H5S36 2008
811'.54—dc22
2007022470

Book design by Julia Gorton and Chad W. Beckerman

Published in 2008 by Abrams Books for Young Readers,
an imprint of Harry N. Abrams, Inc.

Printed and bound in China
10 9 8 7 6 5 4 3 2 1

HNA ▌▌▌ ▌
harry n. abrams, inc.
a subsidiary of La Martinière Groupe
115 West 18th Street
New York, NY 10011
www.hnabooks.com

FOR MY SON, CHIP GHIGNA.
THANK YOU FOR INSPIRING THESE
AND MANY, MANY MORE.

A SPECIAL THANKS TO TAMAR BRAZIS,

AND TO ALL THE KIDS, COACHES, PARENTS,
TEACHERS, LIBRARIANS, AND FRIENDS
OF HOMEWOOD, ALABAMA.
—CG

DAN, YOU SET MORE GOALS THAN ANYONE I KNOW . . .
AND ACTUALLY ACCOMPLISH THEM, BRAVO!
ENDLESS THANKS TO IVY KIRK
AND PAUL KIM, WHO ASSISTED ME WITH THE
ILLUSTRATIONS FOR THIS BOOK.
—JG

Success begins the moment that
You set your goal in place;
Take time to savor every step,
For life is not a race.

GOAL.
MIND

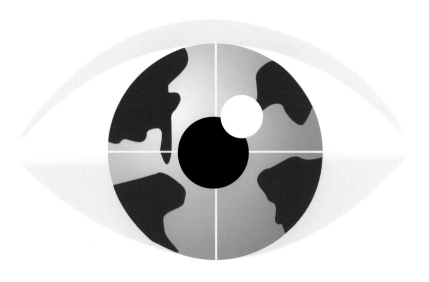

VIEW POINT

Life is grand or life is bland,
It's all in how it's viewed;
The way you see the world depends
Upon your attitude.

THE HIGH ROAD

he path to
nspiration
tarts

Upon
the trails
we've known;

Each
stumbling
block is not
a rock,

But just
a stepping
stone.

IN SIGHT

CLOSE YOUR EYES
AND LOOK INSIDE,
A MIRROR SHINES
WITHIN;
TO FIND WHERE
YOU ARE GOING,
FIRST SEE WHERE
YOU HAVE BEEN.

GOOD MEASURE

Success is often measured best
Not by how high or far,
But what you had to sacrifice
To get to where you are.

UNCOMMON DEEDS

The secret to success is not
To do as everyone;
Success is often measured by
What others haven't done.

TREE OF KNOWLEDGE

The woodpecker has shown us how
A worthy life is led;

We cannot leave
our mark on life
Unless we use
our head.

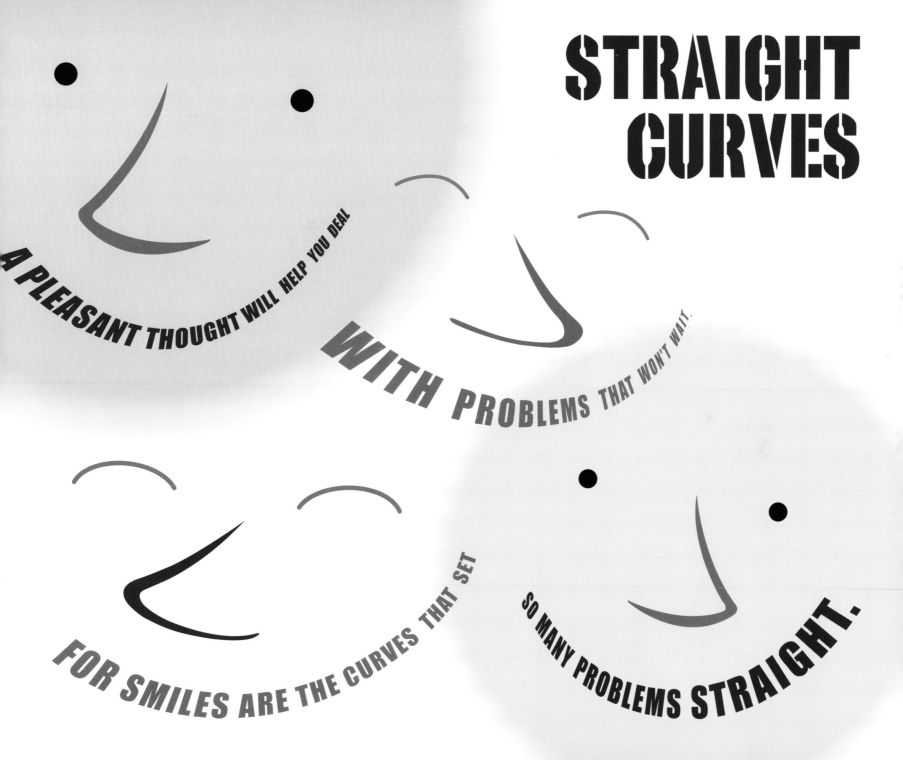

STRAIGHT CURVES

A PLEASANT THOUGHT WILL HELP YOU DEAL

WITH PROBLEMS THAT WON'T WAIT.

FOR SMILES ARE THE CURVES THAT SET

SO MANY PROBLEMS STRAIGHT.

GOAL TENDING

To reach your greatest dreams in life,

First set a worthy goal;

Choose one you can embrace each day

With all your heart and soul.

SURE THING

Good luck is not a random act
Of probability;
It's when your preparation meets
An opportunity.

THAT'S
THE TICKET

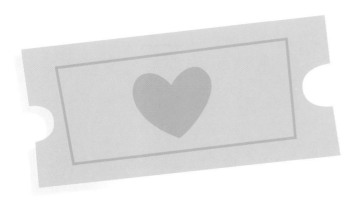

Don't let a negative approach
Tear all your dreams apart.
Your ticket to a happy life?
An optimistic heart.

THE RIGHT TOUCH

A thoughtful word, a thoughtful deed,
We never lose the knack,
For kindness is a boomerang
That always comes right back.

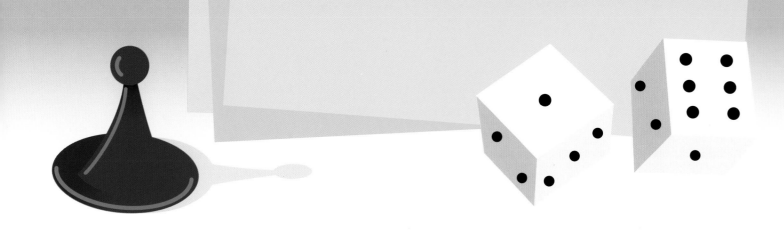

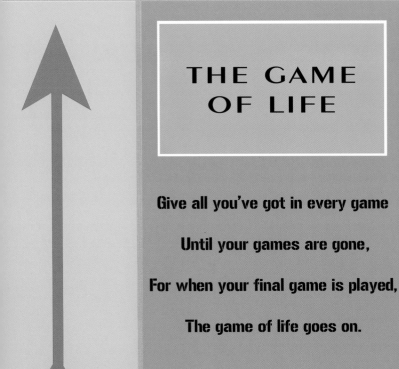

THE GAME OF LIFE

Give all you've got in every game

Until your games are gone,

For when your final game is played,

The game of life goes on.

WORK ETHIC

Self-discipline and you will win
By working hard each day,
For habits that you practice now
Will never go away.

VICTORY CALLS

The way to get victory

To greet you

Is to never let failure

Defeat you.

NEVER GIVE UP

A loss becomes a victory
When you promise not to quit,
But a failure's just a failure
Unless you learn from it.

THE SPIRIT OF PLAY

The final score is more than how

We win or lose with pride;

It's how we play the game of life

With laughter on our side.

TEST PATTERN

Each time our troubles test our will,
We wonder of their use,
Until we learn to keep them from
Becoming an excuse.

ANTS NEVER CRY "UNCLE"

Consider the little ant:
He never says "I can't."
And so it comes as no surprise,
He carries things ten times his size.

THINK TANK

It doesn't take an army
To think what can be done;
One person with just one idea
Is more than ten with none.

LIE

TRUTH

IN THE BLINK OF A LIE

Truth can always catch a lie
With just a steady pace;
Although integrity is slow,
It always wins the race.

THE ART OF START

Don't search for inspiration when you have a task to do; Just start your work and you will see That it will soon find you.

HEAVY METTLE

Adversity is what it takes
To see our goals ascend;
In order for the kite to rise,
It flies against the wind.

LIFE LINES

Life
is
what
you
make
of
it,

However
great
or
small;

It
can
be
used
to
take
up
time—

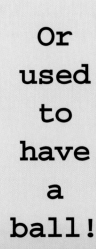

Or
used
to
have
a
ball!

Suitable Language

LANGUAGE IS THE DRESS OF THOUGHT, YOUR WORDS WEAR EVERY SHADE. BE CAREFUL WHAT YOU CHOOSE TO SAY, YOUR MIND IS ON PARADE.

INTEGRITY

It leads us toward the truer path,
It answers many whys,
It shakes the truth out of its sleep
No matter where it lies.

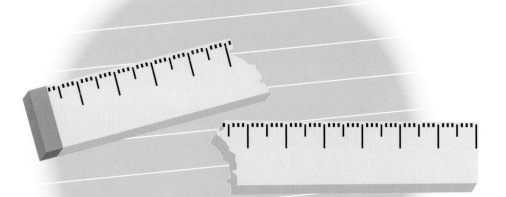

SCHOOL OF HARD KNOCKS

The lesson that some fail to get,
Though all of us should learn it:
Don't think that you deserve your share
Unless you work to earn it.

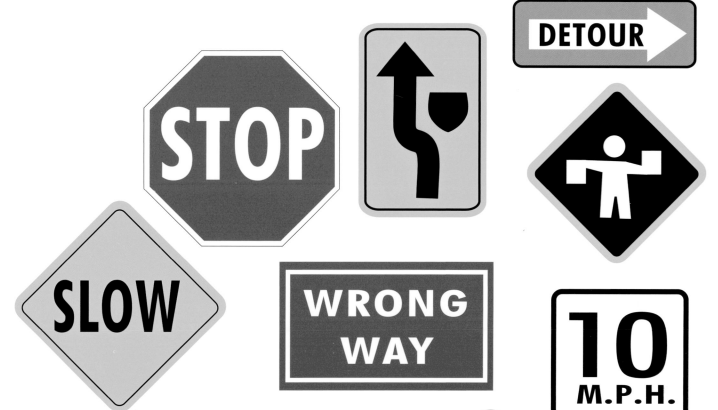

STOP

DETOUR →

WRONG WAY

SLOW

10 M.P.H.

← DETOUR

GOING THE DISTANCE

Success is not an easy road,
It's riddled with resistance,
While failure, on the other hand,
Is the path of least persistence.

DO NOT ENTER

REMEMBER TO FORGET

Achievements
often
come
when
we
forget
our
fears
and
try,
for
that's
when
we
accomplish
what
we're
most
remembered
by.

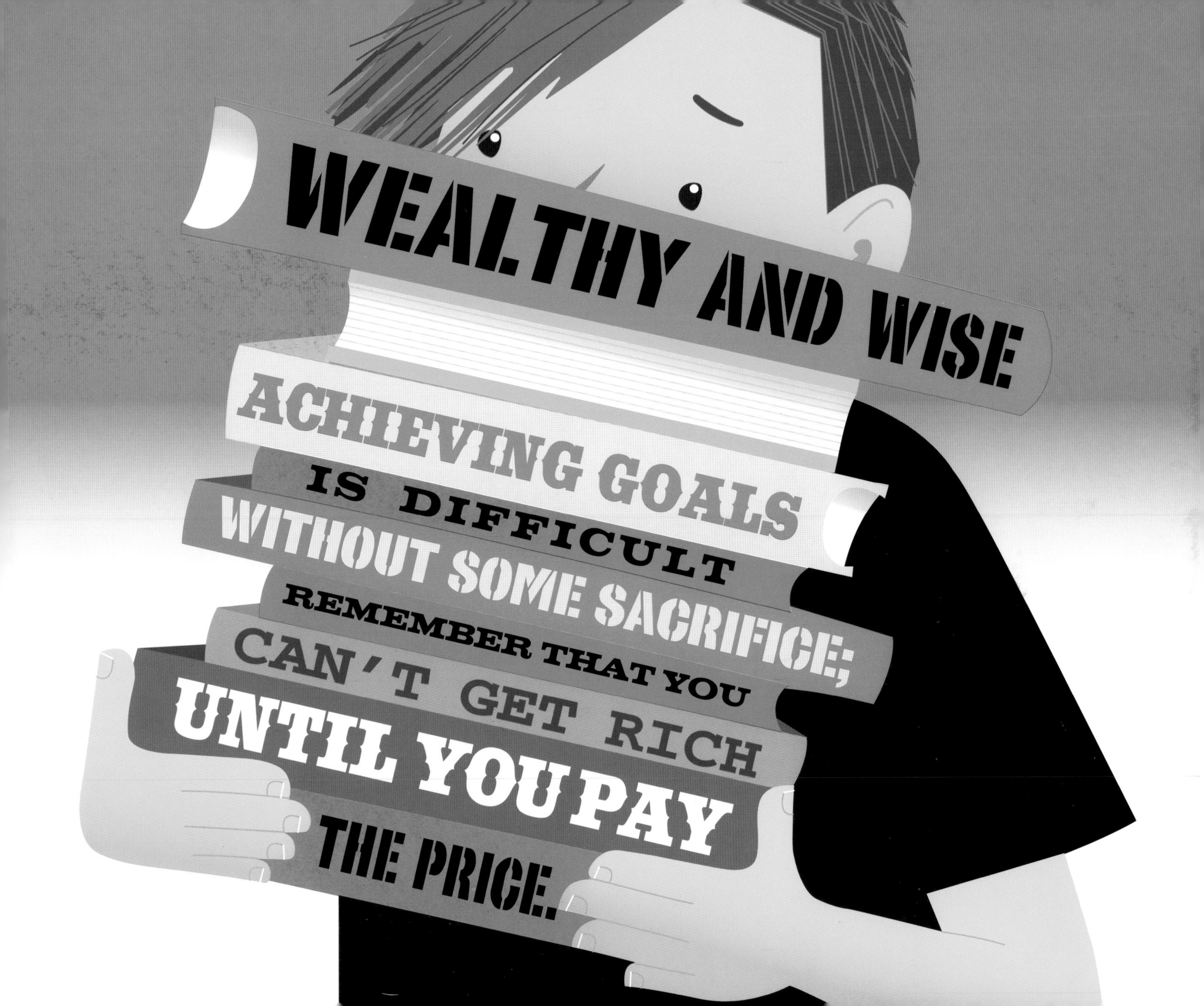
WEALTHY AND WISE
ACHIEVING GOALS
IS DIFFICULT
WITHOUT SOME SACRIFICE;
REMEMBER THAT YOU
CAN'T GET RICH
UNTIL YOU PAY
THE PRICE.

KEY ISSUE

To find the key to your success
Takes more than intuition;
It's not the key that's hard to find,
It's finding the ignition!

SUCCESS FULL

Never doubt what you can do
No matter what the chore;
Success comes when we care enough
To do a little more.

Practice Winning

Winners practice every day,
They do not quit or yield;

Before they win it in the game,
They win it on the field.

Winning Strategy

Self-discipline is what it takes
To find a way to win;

To see if you have what it takes,
Just take a look within.

THE MOVE FROM FAILURE TO SUCCESS TAKES MORE THAN SIMPLY GRIT;

FAILURE TO

SUCCESS

IT STARTS WHEN YOU FIRST REALIZE YOU KNOW YOU'LL NEVER QUIT.

LIGHT TOUCH

There's nothing gray about the truth,
It's simply wrong or right;
For shadows disappear from view
When we stand in the light.

TEST OF CHARACTER

Character is built each time
We face up to the test;
The two most difficult, of course,
Are failure and success.

Allow yourself to fish each day
Within life's little streams,
For that is where we often find
Just how to catch our dreams.

DREAM CATCHER

Giving it Another try

Is better than

An alibi.

KNOW EXCUSES

WORTH A SHOT

A lesson learned from basketball
Is one we all should make:
You always miss all the shots
That you never take.

LESSON IN SUCCESS

If you should dare to try success,
Consider this prerequisite:
First study unsuccessful deeds—
Then go and do the opposite.

DIAMOND MIND

The promise of our dreams comes true
When patience minds our goal;
Remember that the diamond once
Was just a piece of coal.

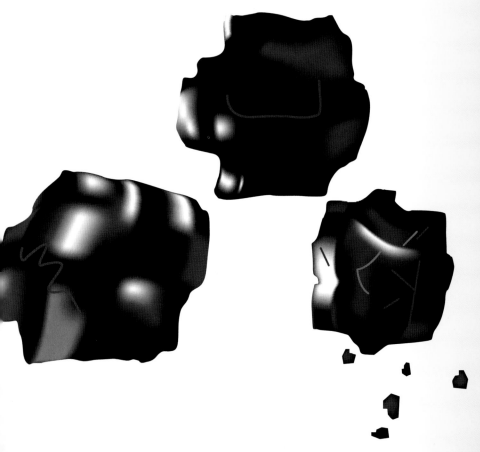

Finish Lines ①

★ ① **Success is never measured by**

② **The things we try to do;** ★

③ **It only comes when we have seen**

④ **A task completely through.** ★

HEADWAY

Do not let fear confine your life
Inside a shell of doubt;
A turtle never moves until
His head is sticking out.

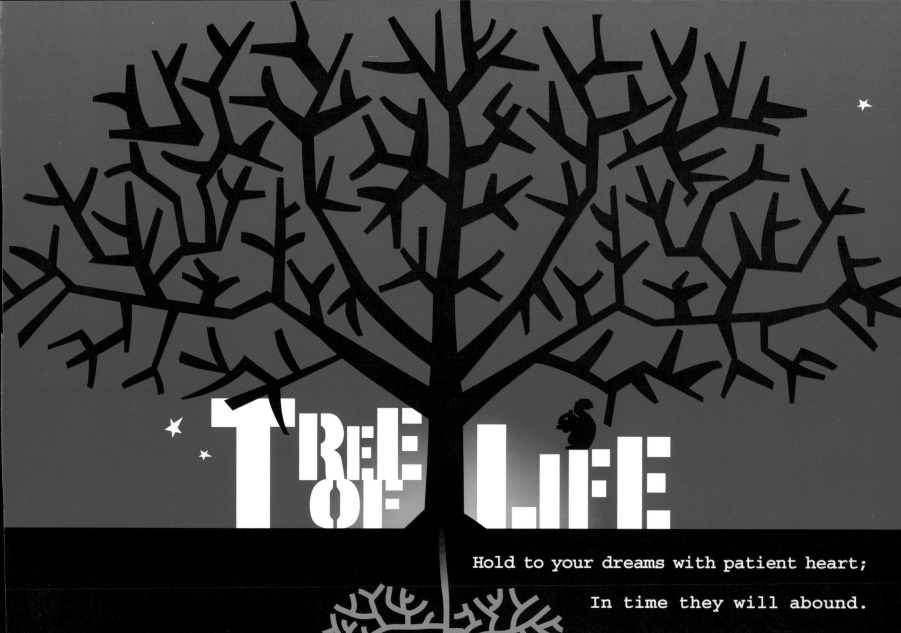

TREE OF LIFE

Hold to your dreams with patient heart;

In time they will abound.

The mighty oak is just a nut

That finally held its ground.

SOLID GOAL.

Don't let the distance to your goals
Keep you from your dreams;
It's never really
quite as far
As what it often
seems.